I0012017

CONTENTS

INTRODUCTION

The inspiration for this book is my not-so-tech-savvy mother and father-in-law!

The aim is to help you understand what you're holding in your hand, how powerful it can be and how best to configure it before you even start exploring your smartphone and organising your life!

By the end of the book, you will be thinking of many ways to make the most of your smartphone and be confident about your online security and safety in general.

Let's get into the basics so that we're on the same page.

THE BASICS

SO, WHAT IS A SMARTPHONE?

A Smartphone is simply the combination of a traditional mobile phone with advanced computing capabilities.

WHAT IS A SMARTPHONE USEFUL FOR?

A smartphone can be used to organise all of your daily activities, keep track of tasks and routines, communicate easily with family and friends, store important documents and information and entertain you!

WHAT IS ANDROID?

Android is what some smartphones use to run all its logic, computations and communications and to display those in an easy to view format. The technical term is an Operating System. There are other Operating Systems for mobile phones, such as iOS (used in Apple smartphones), however this guide will be focusing on Android-related usage.

WHAT IS THE CLOUD?

In the context of this book, data and information storage. Think of the cloud like a personal, private and secure locker storing a copy of your phone data.

QUICK REFERENCE

As you read through this book, you'll come across instructions to search for apps or settings or perform some actions on your smartphone. You can reference the below to kick start your knowledge on where to look and how to search.

SEARCHING FOR SETTINGS

There are generally two ways to search for settings:

1. Swipe From The Top

   1) Swipe down from the top of the phone (usually from the clock works)

   2) Tap on the Cog/Wheel (usually in the top right)

   3) Tap on the magnifying glass (usually top right)

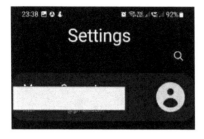

4) Type in the word/s your searching for (follow the instructions)

2. Find The Settings Icon

1) Swipe up from the bottom of the phone (try starting from between the square and "<")

2) This will show your installed apps along with the Settings icon which looks like:

FINDING APPS

1) Swipe up from the bottom of the phone (try starting from between the square and "<")

2) This will show your installed apps
3) Tap on the Search bar (usually right at the top)

4) Start typing the name of the app you're looking for

LOCKING YOUR PHONE

Depending on the type of phone you have, the lock button (which is a physical button) could be across the top of the phone or on the side of the phone (sometimes below the volume controls). If all else fails, hit each physical button individually see what happens!

SECURITY AND PRIVACY

In this day and age, online security and privacy is paramount to having a safe and great online experience. The following steps will explain the first actions you need to take before you even start using and exploring your phone.

SCREEN LOCK

This is when you are not using your phone and want to make sure that it doesn't accidentally get knocked and unwittingly make a call to your boss or daughter while having a few drinks at the party. It is also useful to prevent any unwanted characters accessing your personal information such as your emails, documents and bank account info.

SCREEN LOCK OPTIONS

For the screen lock to be useful, you'll need to decide how you want to unlock your screen when the time comes. Many phones these days have an option for using your fingerprints in conjunction with either a password or pattern in case your fingers are wet or the phone doesn't recognise them for some reason. You can also simply have a pin, password or pattern without using your fingerprints.

My recommendation would be to setup your fingerprints as your first priority, with a pattern or password as its backup. There are two main reasons for my recommendation: 1) It's much faster to pull your finger out and place it on the screen than typing in a pin, password or drawing a pattern (in my experience), 2) Many applications that have sensitive data, such as online banking, tax software and trading, will have an option to use your fingerprint to login rather than requiring a password. Again, this makes it easier, faster to login and is less likely for access to fall into the wrong hands.

Whichever way you choose to secure your phone, DO NOT SHARE your pin, password, pattern or fingers with anyone. Also, don't write them down (or chop them off) and store them in your dresser drawer. Treat your phone and security method like it's your bank card (when you have to take money out or use a PIN if tap and go don't work!). Note: You will need to remember your pin, password or pattern as you'll need them after turning your phone back on after it has been switched off or when the battery runs out.

STEPS TO SETUP YOUR LOCK SCREEN SECURITY

If you haven't already done this when you first set up your phone or for some reason the settings have been reset and/or you want to change the settings, follow the steps below:

1) Swipe down from the top of the phone (usually from the clock works)
2) Tap on the Cog/Wheel in the top right
3) Go down to Security and privacy
4) Tap on Lock screen (you may need to enter a pin, password or pattern)
5) Choose the Screen lock type

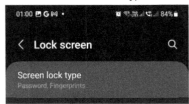

6) You can set up all of the below but can only have one as your screen lock at a time
    a) **PIN** - Medium-high security as it's sometimes harder for dodgy people to remember numbers than a pattern. It is recommended to have a pin that is 6 digits or longer - the more numbers in a PIN the better!
    b) **Password** - High security as it is even harder for those nasty characters to remember when watching over your shoulder; make sure that you have at least 8 characters and a combination of lowercase letters, uppercase letters, numbers and special characters (like #, $ and %). I find an easy way to create long passwords is to use a favourite song and use the first letter of each word while

converting some to numbers or special characters. For example, "Islands in the stream, that is what we are, no one in between" could translate to: iitsTiwwaN1!b

c) **Pattern** - Medium security as it's a bit easier for those pesky peepers to remember.

DO NOT choose Swipe or None. This is not secure at all.

7) After you have set your PIN, password or pattern, it's now time to enable your fingerprints. Tap "Fingerprints" or the switch on the right hand side. If you haven't already registered your fingerprints, it will prompt you to register them; follow the prompts to register.

8) You can enable Face too, but that is entirely up to you!

If you have already registered fingerprints and want to add more (or edit existing fingers as they may have new scars that muck up the scanning), follow these steps:

1) Follow steps 1-3 above

2) Under Lock screen; Tap "Fingerprints"

3) You will need to enter your PIN, password or pattern that you configured previously

4) Tap "Add fingerprint" to add a fingerprint, or tap on an existing fingerprint to rename it or to remove it

5) Adding a fingerprint can take a minute or two; make sure that you follow the instructions and cover as much of the fingerprint as possible (slightly different angles, different edges, etc.); a progress indicator will show how far you're into the process.

Note: I recommend adding two or more fingers, especially if there are different ways you pick up the phone.

ENABLE FIND MY PHONE

If you need to find your phone, whether it be you who has misplaced it or has been taken accidentally or intentionally, you can enable the service on your phone. Depending on the phone manufacturer, there are slightly different ways this is done. The best way to enable this is to:

1) Swipe down from the top of the phone (usually from the clock works)
2) Tap on the Cog/Wheel in the top right
3) Tap on the magnifying glass (usually top right)
4) Type in "Find my"
5) Look through the search results and tap the most appropriate
6) Follow the prompts (below is an example from a Samsung smartphone)

ADD A RECOVERY EMAIL ADDRESS AND CONTACT

If you have forgotten your password and can no longer access your Google data (e.g. emails, calendar and documents), you can configure a recovery email address and contact. This should be someone that you trust and ideally doesn't have access to your email. It could be another account that you have setup which you manage, but the risk of doing that is if you forget the password for that one too, you're in trouble!

The best way to get this configured is to go to your Google account settings by:

1) Go to your phone settings - sometimes by swiping down from the top of the phone (usually from the clock works) and tapping on the Cog/ Wheel in the top right; you can also search for settings by going to your apps (usually swiping up) and searching for settings

2) Find Accounts (sometimes Accounts and backup) and tap it

3) Find Manage accounts and tap

4) Look for your Google account (you may have several accounts on your phone depending on how many applications you have and if they store account information on your phone). Look out for the "G" and your email address next to it

5) Tap on your account

6) Tap on "Google Account"; this will take you to a view of your account, including Account Storage and other information

7) Look for and tap on Security by swiping left on the line that has "Home", "Personal Info" and other headings

8) Scroll down to see your security information, including your Recovery phone and Recovery email

9) Add or update as required

BACKING UP YOUR PHONE AND DATA

As you'll be using your phone to store important information such as bills, contacts, appointments, photos, text messages, phone call history and other documents, it's very important to backup your data in case your phone is stolen, broken, lost and/or erased. It also makes it much easier to transfer to another phone or device at a later time.

There are many ways to backup your phone, including the phone manufacturer's backup application and other options like Backup by Google One which is built-in to the Android phone. The phone manufacturer's backup software generally will only work with the same brand mobile phones if you need to restore your data, whereas Google backups will be able to work with other Android mobile phones as long as they have the same or later Android version.

The easiest way to backup the majority of your information is to use the Google sync option as it doesn't rely on the phone manufacturer. If you decide to change from an HTC to a Samsung, for example, you'll setup the phone with your Google account and it'll start synchronising your contacts, appointments, emails, etc. from the cloud.

Check Storage

One thing to check when selecting Backup by Google One is that you have enough Account storage. When you follow the steps below, it should tell you how much Account storage you are using and how much storage you have been allocated/purchased.

If you have a standard Google account, you are allocated 15GB* of storage which goes across all Google services such as Email, Drive and Photos. Depending on how you use your phone and Google account in general, including how many photos you take, how many emails you receive and how you use Google Drive (document storage which I'll take you through in Chapter 4), you may need to consider purchasing additional storage. To get additional storage, along with other benefits, go to https://one.google.com/about/plans and follow the prompts.

*To give you an idea on how much data 15GB is, it is about 6500 high quality photos; you can fit the entire works of Shakespeare in 5MB (0.005GB).

STEPS TO CONFIGURE BACKUP BY GOOGLE ONE

1) Swipe down from the top of the phone (usually from the clock works)

2) Tap on the Cog/Wheel in the top right

3) Scroll down to Accounts and Backup

4) Under the "Google Drive" section, tap Back up data

5) Follow the prompts to configure

MULTI-FACTOR AUTHENTICATION (MFA)

You may have heard the acronym two-factor authentication, MFA or the whole term multi-factor authentication. This simply means that rather than having a single way (also known as factor) to prove you are who you "say" you are, you have two or more; and to take it a little step further, it's usually something that you know (like a password or PIN) and something that you have (like a random token generator or a text message that you receive with a code).

The single factor you may be used to are passwords. Many websites ask for a username and password and once you enter both, they let you in. As soon as someone finds out your password, they can then access that website and appear to be you.

In the online world, this is a VERY important thing to understand and set up wherever and whenever you can. This will help provide a higher level of security for your financial, personal and private information and prevent those nasty characters from getting access.

There are different ways of providing a second factor, with the most common nowadays being a text or email message containing a temporary or one-time code (also known as One-Time Password or OTP). It is unlikely that a nasty character will have both your username/password combination AND access to your phone/text messages.

Another method which is not as common but is more secure than a text message is secure tokens. This usually requires an app on your phone which generates random codes on time intervals (usually expire and regenerate a new one every minute). To access the app and the codes, you will need to enter your phone's chosen method/s of security such as your password, pattern or fingerprint.

Seeing as you're on an Android and have a Google account, I would recommend downloading Google Authenticator from the Google Play store. It's easy to set up initially and will be ready for you when you get to a website or app that has the option of using secure authentication tokens. The instructions will be in the app or website and are usually easy to follow.

There are other applications and services that have their own secure authentication service, like Government applications, which you would need to download and set up following their specific instructions. As mentioned earlier, it is VERY important to understand and set up to have the most secure access to your information.

If you're worried that you may forget how to use the secure authentication application or service, applications and websites will have another way to recover from that scenario. When you first setup the app/website, it should ensure that you have alternative, but secure, ways to recover, such as adding a phone number to your profile which can receive temporary passwords/codes.

SAFETY

An added benefit of carrying a smartphone is that you can use its advanced features for your safety. Sometimes you may get lost and have no idea which way to go to get to safety or a familiar place, other times you may be in a situation where you are in danger and need to reach out for help and other times you may not be able to provide critical information to first responders.

The next few pages show some ways to help!

MEDICAL INFORMATION

Hopefully you don't have an emergency where you can't respond to first responders or other people trying to help you, such as having an anaphylactic reaction, heart attack, stroke, concussion, etc. but if you do end up in a situation like this, it would be great for people to know some key medical information, right? Things like any allergies, conditions, medications, blood type and other info.

This info is shown on the lock screen by default which you can switch off but still have ready at hand in case you forget key information yourself (has happened to me a few times such as my blood type!).

To add your emergency information:

1) Go to your phone settings - sometimes by swiping down from the top of the phone (usually from the clock works) and tapping on the Cog/Wheel in the top right; you can also search for settings by going to your apps (usually swiping up) and searching for settings

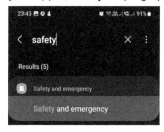

2) Find and tap Safety and Emergency

3) Tap on Medical info

4) Fill out the fields as you wish

5) Tap Save

Note: If you don't want this info to display on your Lock screen, tap on the switch/toggle

If you have opted to show your medical information on the lock screen, you can see what's there by:

1)   Locking your phone

2)   Double tapping or hitting the lock button

3)   Swipe in any direction

4)   Tap on Emergency Call

5)   Tap on Medical info

EMERGENCY CONTACTS

Emergency contacts are people you trust to help you in an emergency. They'll be contacted if you start emergency sharing. You can also show them on the Lock screen for quick access in an emergency.

To add Emergency Contacts:

1) Go to your phone settings - sometimes by swiping down from the top of the phone (usually from the clock works) and tapping on the Cog/ Wheel in the top right; you can also search for settings by going to your apps (usually swiping up) and searching for settings

2) Find and tap Safety and Emergency

3) Tap on Emergency contacts

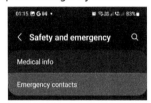

4) Scroll down and tap on "Add emergency contact"

5) This will bring up your contacts list; look for the appropriate contact and tap on them. This will add them to the list at the top of the screen.

6) Repeat step 5 as required

7) Once all have been selected, tap "Done"
You will now see the list on the screen

8) You can also show your emergency contacts on the Lock screen by tapping the switch next to "Show on Lock screen"

SHARING YOUR LOCATION WITH LOVED ONES

There may be an occasion where you need help navigating out of an area from someone who knows the area or even someone that has access to a detailed map. Another instance may be if you're on a road trip and want to let your family know your whereabouts as you travel along.

The simplest way to do this on an Android smartphone is to go into the pre-installed "Maps"application, then:

1) Tap on your profile picture (or it could be your initials) in the top right of the screen

2) Tap Location Sharing

3) At this point you may be prompted to give extra permissions to the application to allow sharing your location; follow the prompts and select the appropriate permission, e.g.

    a)   Allow all the time - this will ensure that people you share your location with will be able to see your location regardless of whether you're using the Maps application or not (note: this may use up your battery faster when you are sharing your location with people)

b)   Allow only while using the app - if you want to keep your location somewhat private but still be able to share your location, you can choose this option which will only share your location when you have the Maps application open

4) Tap on the icon on the bottom right - it looks like a person with a plus (+) sign next to them

5) You may need to allow Maps to access your contacts - tap Allow

6) Tap Continue if you are prompted with more information (e.g. "Stay connected")

7) Select the option for sharing your real-time location

   a) For 1 hour - you can extend the number of hours as required; this is useful if you are going on a road trip or a long drive

   b)   Until you turn this off - this may be useful for loved ones that may be concerned about you; perhaps you've just returned home from an operation and may be unstable. Afterall, you need to get out of the house at some point even if it may be a little scary and you have the potential of falling over and not accessing your phone

8) The smartphone will suggest some contacts that you may be in touch with often. In this case, select the appropriate person. If they aren't on that list, swipe to the left on one of the names until you get to "More".

9) This will show people from your Contacts; tap on the person/people, then tap Send

10) The people you have selected will receive an email stating that you have opted to share your location with them and give them a link/button to allow your invitation.

11) Next time you are sharing your location, your selected contacts can open up the "Maps" app on their phone or through a browser and find out where you are.

SENDING FOR HELP

There may be occasions where you are in a compromising situation where you need to make a call for help to Emergency services or even trusted people in your life that can help in an emergency. There are an infinite number of reasons for needing emergency assistance such as falling over and being unable to use the phone correctly; getting chased by unknown nasty characters and other unthinkable situations. Apart from calling the emergency services number directly or contacting loved ones directly, there are a number of options to set up and use your smartphone to reach out in the event of an emergency, these are listed below:

EMERGENCY SHARING

Emergency sharing sends your current location and request for help to your emergency contacts. It then lets them know if your location changes or your battery runs low. Note: You can Start emergency sharing immediately or by tapping the lock button 5 times.

To see and/or change the settings:

1) Go to your phone settings - sometimes by swiping down from the top of the phone (usually from the clock works) and tapping on the Cog/ Wheel in the top right; you can also search for settings by going to your apps (usually swiping up) and searching for settings

2) Find and tap Safety and Emergency

3) Tap on Emergency sharing

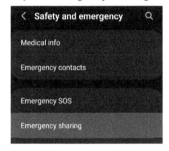

4) Attach pictures (optional):

Takes pictures with the front and rear cameras and include them in your messages

5) Attach audio recording (optional):

Record 5 seconds of audio and include it in your messages

CALLING EMERGENCY SERVICES BY PRESSING
THE LOCK BUTTON MULTIPLE TIMES

You can set up your phone to call your country's emergency services by pressing the lock button on the side of your phone 5 times (this is a hard coded number). Note: some smartphones may already have this enabled by default; it came out a couple of years back in a software update and cannot be disabled.

Steps:

1) Go to your phone settings - sometimes by swiping down from the top of the phone (usually from the clock works) and tapping on the Cog/ Wheel in the top right; you can also search for settings by going to your apps (usually swiping up) and use the search bar

2) Find and tap Safety and Emergency

3) Tap on Emergency SOS

4) Countdown (optional):
   You can have the phone immediately phone emergency services or you can have a countdown of 10 seconds (useful if kids often play with your phone - Note: pressing the lock button that number of times can be an honest mistake/accident (or a grandchild/child picks up the phone and plays with it - it happens, trust me!*)

5) Play warning sound (optional):
   This will play a loud sound when the SOS has been activated; again,

it's good to have if you have kids around, but the downside is that it won't be useful if you are in a compromising situation where you need to make an inconspicuous call to emergency services.

6) Emergency number to call:

Make sure the correct Emergency Services number for your country/ area is there or put in a custom number (you may have a personal emergency service that you would like to contact)

7) Share info with emergency contacts (optional):

You may want to share your location and a message to people you have selected as emergency contacts on your phone; the info to share is configured in Emergency sharing.

---

*My 4 year old son hit the lock button a lot of times which resulted in calling emergency services. The conversation went as follows: "Ambulance, Fire or Police?", son: "I don't know"; responder: "Are you in danger?", son: "I don't know". My son then hands over the phone to me without saying anything; I see emergency services on the phone and hang up in a panic. They call back and ask if everything's alright and I confirm that everything was and it was a mistake.

SET UP YOUR
ESSENTIAL APPS

EMAIL

Email is still one of the most important tools in your arsenal for communication and organisation. Being on an Android phone, you'll notice that Gmail is installed and most likely your default email app.

If you have other email addresses that aren't with Google, feel free to download the app related to that provider (e.g. Outlook for Microsoft email addresses). You can easily switch between email apps as required, however my personal recommendation is to use Gmail with your Google account as it has tighter and built-in integration with your Android phone.

Gmail, and other email apps, allow you to create labels that you can apply to emails to make them easier to find after you're done with them initially.

Think of labels as folders or dividers in a filing cabinet with one minor difference - you can divide those folders into smaller folders. For example, rather than having a folder containing all your home-related bills such as electricity, gas, rates, etc. you can create sub-folders. For example, you may have Home/Electricity, Home/Gas, Home/Rates. Believe it or not, this can make it easier to find things as you won't have a huge list of main folders that contain a lot of emails.

Now, open up your email app of choice and access your emails. If it isn't your default email app, you will be asked if you want to make it your default app for emails.

Regardless of your email provider, I highly recommend the use of labels to organise your emails so that once you're done with them in your primary inbox, you can file them away for easier access later.

DOCUMENT MANAGEMENT

Document management can be done easily on your smartphone. Why would I want to use my smartphone for document management? You can easily whip out your smartphone when you have spare time and file things on the move. Why would I want to use an online app for document management and why can't I just keep the documents in my email or save them directly to the phone? The benefit of using an online app for document management is that they will be available on the cloud from any device, including if you lose your phone and/or change to another device in the future, including your laptop.

If you start receiving your bills electronically (which will be one of the topics of my next book), for example, you'll want to keep these in a strict order for future reference. This is especially important for documents that are related to tax returns and other ongoing financial processes; it's so much easier and quicker to find information when it is filed in a structured way.

While there are many apps out there that can provide you with document management functionality, I believe it's always good to stick with a single provider for your information especially when you're on a smartphone. In this case, you guessed it, Google have an app for that which is simply called Drive.

In a similar fashion to Email labels mentioned earlier, Drive has folders which can contain subfolders. A perfect example of this would be creating a folder called "Tax" and have sub-folders for the tax years. Those subfolders can also have their own subfolders and so on. For example, if you have two jobs, you can create a folder for each job under the tax year. There are so many ways you can structure your folders and it's totally flexible.

To get the Drive app, if it's not already installed on your smartphone:1) Go to the Google Play store (you can search for "play" in your apps); it is also usually in a "Google" folder where you look for your installed applications

(swipe up from the bottom of the phone screen)

1) In the search bar, type "Google Drive"
   This will show up as "Google Drive" with Google LLC below it (make sure as you may install a "Drive" app from another company)

2) If it's already installed, it may require an update in which case tap "Update"; if it's not installed:

3) Tap Install next to the app
   Wait for the app to download and install; you will know when it has completed when you have the option to "Open"

4) Tap Open

5) **Allow** Drive to send you notifications (tap Allow)

6) You will then be taken to the Drive app - play around with it to learn (check out my next book to get the most out of Drive!)

CONTACTS

Contacts are the way you communicate with your friends, family and acquaintances. With an Android smartphone, in my opinion, the best way to ensure that your contacts are synchronised and accessible in your other applications is to use the Google Contacts app. Some phones may already have this pre-installed

Steps:

1) Go to the Google Play store (you can search for "play" in your apps); it is also usually in a "Google" folder where you look for your installed applications (swipe up from the bottom of the phone screen)

2) In the search bar, type "Google Contacts"
   This will show up as "Contacts" with Google LLC below it (make sure as you may install a contacts app from another company)

3) Tap Install next to the app
   Wait for the app to download and install; you will know when it has completed when you have the option to "Open"

4) Tap Open

5) **Allow** Contacts to access your contacts (tap Allow)

6) **Allow** Contacts to make and manage phone calls (tap Allow)

7) You will then be taken to the Contact app - play around with it to learn!

MESSAGES (TEXT/SMS)

This app is used for sending and receiving text messages. The majority of smartphone manufacturers come with their own version of a messaging app, however if you're using Backup for Google One as recommended earlier in this book, it is also recommended to use Google Messages to allow easier backups and recoveries when needed. To get the Google Messages app and set it up:

1) Go to the Google Play store (you can search for "play" in your apps); it is also usually in a "Google" folder where you look for your installed applications (swipe up from the bottom of the phone screen)

2) In the search bar, type "Google Messages"
   This will show up as "Google Messages" with Google LLC below it (make sure as you may install a messages app from another company)

3) Tap Install next to the app
   Wait for the app to download and install; you will know when it has completed when you have the option to "Open"

4) Tap Open

5) **Allow** Google Messages to access your contacts (tap Allow)

6) **Allow** Google Messages to make and manage phone calls (tap Allow)

7) **Allow** Google Messages to access Music and audio (tap Allow)

8) **Allow** Google Messages to send Notifications (tap Allow)

9) **Allow** Google Messages to access Photos and videos (tap Allow)

10) **Allow** Google Messages to access SMS (tap Allow)

11) You will then be taken to the Google Messages app - play around with it to learn!

CALENDAR

Calendar is your appointment and simple task tracking app. You can use it to invite others in your contacts to events and more importantly use it to set up reminders for important events. The majority of smartphone manufacturers come with their own version of a calendar app, however if you're using Backup for Google One as recommended earlier in this book, it is also recommended to use Google Calendar to allow easier backups and recoveries when needed. It is also useful for keeping your Calendar in sync when moving between devices such as tablets and laptops. To get Google Calendar:

1) Go to the Google Play store (you can search for "play" in your apps); it is also usually in a "Google" folder where you look for your installed applications (swipe up from the bottom of the phone screen)

2) In the search bar, type "Google Calendar"
   This will show up as "Google Calendar" with Google LLC below it (make sure as you may install a calendar app from another company)

3) Tap Install next to the app
   Wait for the app to download and install; you will know when it has completed when you have the option to "Open"

4) Tap Open

5) **Allow** Google Calendar to access your contacts (tap Allow)

6) **Allow** Google Calendar to access your Contacts (tap Allow)

7) **Allow** Google Calendar to access your location (tap Always, Only when using app or never)

8) **Allow** Google Calendar to send Notifications (tap Allow)

9) You will then be taken to the Google Calendar app - play around with it to learn!

CONCLUSION

I hope that my book has helped you understand how important security is in this online world especially when it comes to your smartphone, how to secure your smartphone as well as giving you a helping hand getting set up and ready to go.

Now that you're all secure and configured for productivity, get ready to get organised!

My second book will be about how to use your smartphone for organising your life, including how to organise and streamline those pesky bills - especially those that are still coming in the mail!

If you found this book helpful, I'd be very appreciative if you left a favourable review for the book on Amazon!

REFERENCES

How your Google storage works - Gmail Help. (n.d.).

https://support.google.com/mail/answer/9312312?hl=en

Plans & pricing - Google One. (n.d.). Google One.

https://one.google.com/about/plans

Keheley, P. (n.d.). *How many pages in a gigabyte? A litigator's guide.* https://

www.digitalwarroom.com/blog/how-many-pages-in-a-gigabyte